Table of Contents

"As our culture collapses around us, the issues of bioethics lie at the heart of its crisis. And why? Because they address the foundational questions of human nature, and every culture is premised on its own assumptions about what it means to be human.

"In this series these extraordinary questions are tackled with due seriousness (they make everyone think) and yet also with accessibility (no one who thinks will be excluded). It is hard to imagine a more important set of questions or a more timely publication."

Nigel M. de S. Cameron, Ph.D.
Provost, Trinity International University

"These booklets are packed with information and moral insights that will provide needed help to pastors, health care professionals, and teachers seeking direction in the ever-changing world of bioethics. Nothing less than human dignity hangs in the balance."

Francis J. Beckwith, Ph.D.
Associate Professor of Philosophy, Culture, and Law
Trinity Graduate School and Trinity Law School
Trinity International University

The BioBasics Series provides insightful and practical answers to many of today's pressing bioethical questions. Advances in medical technology have resulted in longer and healthier lives, but they have also produced interventions and procedures that call for serious ethical evaluation. What we can do is not necessarily what we should do. This series is designed to instill in each reader an uncompromising respect for human life that will serve as a compass through a maze of challenging questions.

This series is a project of The Center for Bioethics and Human Dignity, an international organization located just north of Chicago, Illinois, in the United States of America. The Center endeavors to bring Christian perspectives to bear on today's many difficult bioethical challenges. It develops book, audio tape, and video tape series; presents numerous conferences in different parts of the world; and offers a variety of other printed and computer-based resources. Through its membership program, the Center provides world-wide resources on bioethical matters. Members receive the Center's international journal, *Ethics and Medicine,* the Center's newsletter, *Dignity,* the Center's *Update Letters,* special World Wide Web access, an Internet News Service and Discussion Forum, and discounts on most bioethics resources in print.

For more information on membership in the Center or its various resources, including present or future books in the BioBasics Series, contact the Center at:

The Center for Bioethics and Human Dignity
2065 Half Day Road
Bannockburn, IL 60015 USA
Phone: (847) 317-8180 Fax: (847) 317-8153
E-mail: cbhd@banninst.edu

Information and ordering is also available through the Center's World Wide Web site on the Internet: http://www.bioethix.org

BioBasics Series

Basic Questions on
Sexuality and Reproductive Technology

When Is It Right to Intervene?

Gary P. Stewart, D.Min.
William R. Cutrer, M.D.
Timothy J. Demy, Th.D.
Dónal P. O'Mathúna, Ph.D.
Paige C. Cunningham, J.D.
John F. Kilner, Ph.D.
Linda K. Bevington, M. A.

kregel
PUBLICATIONS

Grand Rapids, MI 49501

Contributors

Linda K. Bevington, M.A., is the Project Manager for the Center for Bioethics and Human Dignity, Bannockburn, Illinois.

Paige C. Cunningham, J.D., has written numerous articles on abortion and the law; she is a coauthor of the amicus brief that Justice O'Connor cited in her discussion of viability in *Webster v. Reproductive Health Services.*

William R. Cutrer, M.D., served for many years as an obstetrician/gynecologist specializing in the treatment of infertility. He is currently serving as the Dallas/Fort Worth Area Director for The Christian Medical and Dental Society.

Timothy J. Demy, Th.M., Th.D., is a military chaplain and coauthor and author of numerous books and articles. He is a member of the Evangelical Theological Society.

John F. Kilner, Ph.D., is Director of the Center for Bioethics and Human Dignity, Bannockburn, Illinois. He is also Professor of Bioethics and Contemporary Culture at Trinity International University, Deerfield, Illinois.

Dónal P. O'Mathúna, Ph.D., is Associate Professor of Medical Ethics and Chemistry at Mount Carmel College of Nursing, Columbus, Ohio.

Gary P. Stewart, Th.M., D.Min., is a military chaplain and coauthor of numerous books and articles. He is a member of the Evangelical Theological Society.

Introduction

Medical interventions used to help people fight against cancer are lauded as great scientific discoveries. So are technologies that help people survive serious injury or defeat the many viruses that threaten humanity. But what about medical research and intervention that seeks to overcome an individual's apparent inability to produce children? Is infertility a health issue that may be medically corrected? Or, is it always a condition produced by God and, therefore, outside the bounds of medical research?

The authors believe that infertility is a health issue that, like any other health issue, can be addressed with the guidance of an all-knowing and merciful God. Therefore, those of us who pursue having children should do so in a manner that respects God's purposes for marriage, parenthood, and sexuality. Going to great lengths to satisfy our desire or sense of calling to have children may well be appropriate.

In the process, however, we must protect our own well-being and the lives of our children at every stage of their development. Regardless of the outcome, our faith in and dependence on God should not waver but be strengthened through whatever morally acceptable avenue we may pursue. In a fallen world that is too often unjust and cruel, God knows what is best.

As in the case with all decisions, not only those involving childbearing, our heart attitude should reflect the words of Proverbs:

Trust in the LORD with all your heart
And do not lean on your own understanding.
In all your ways acknowledge Him,
And He will make your paths straight.

(Prov. 3:5–6)

This book is not intended to reproduce all the available information on the subject but rather to simplify, complement, and supplement other available sources that the reader is encouraged to consult. Some of these materials have been listed at the end of this book. This book is not intended to take the place of theological, legal, medical, or psychological counsel or treatment. If assistance in any of these areas is needed, please seek the services of a certified professional. The views expressed in this work are solely those of the authors and do not represent or reflect the position or endorsement of any governmental agency or department, military or otherwise.

1. Why do people turn to various forms of assisted reproduction?

Approximately 15 percent of couples desiring to have children are unable to do so after one year of normal marital relations. According to the most common definition of fertility, such couples are infertile. More couples suffer from infertility today than ever before, for a variety of reasons. Some delay attempts at conception until later in life when fertility rates decline. Others suffer the consequences of sexually transmitted diseases that can cause difficulties with conception and completing a pregnancy. When infertility occurs, some sort of intervention is needed for conception to take place.

People will go to great lengths to conceive a child for the longing to have a child is a powerful drive. A biblical list of things never satisfied includes a "barren womb" (Prov. 30:16). The need for children mentioned here is a generalization, not a mandate for each individual woman; however, it does suggest that the desire for a child can be intense and ongoing. Therefore, many couples, unable to conceive naturally, seek guidance from the theological community and assistance from the medical community. A theistic worldview allows for the perspective that God has permitted major medical advances. Such advances provide considerable insight into the complexities of the fertilization process. Those who do not believe in God also generally applaud research and human ingenuity in recognizing and solving reproductive problems. Many medications and procedures are currently available to assist couples in fulfilling the desire for children. Thus, people turn to assisted reproduction to continue the family line or family name, to contribute to the next generation, or simply to fill their homes with a child's love.

From a Christian worldview, each of the available technologies must be understood accurately in light of biblical principles, with due attention given to the sanctity of human life.

2. Is infertility my fault?

Infertility is the inability either to conceive after one year of unprotected intercourse or to carry a conception beyond the first trimester (twelve menstrual weeks).

Infertility in the United States can be traced to the following sources: In one-third of so-called infertile couples, the man has a diagnosed medical problem; in one-third the problem is the woman's; and in the remaining third, there are difficulties with both partners. But, in fact, for a small percentage of couples, no medical abnormality can be detected. Historically, when couples suffered with infertility, it was assumed that the woman was the source of the medical problem. Experts assumed that if a man could sustain an erection and ejaculate, he was "fertile." Precise testing and better understanding of the many variables involved in infertility have demonstrated fertility's complexity. Fortunately, many of the diagnosable problems causing infertility can be treated effectively.

Are infertility problems the person's fault? Often, they are not. For example, hormonal problems and imbalances, low sperm counts, genetic abnormalities, and immunologic incompatibilities are typically not the fault of the patient. However, certain sexually transmitted diseases such as gonorrhea and chlamydia may result from either spouse's premarital or extramarital sexual relationships and may lead to tubal damage and infertility. Decisions to delay attempts at pregnancy until later in life may also play a role.

While the Bible is not a textbook on infertility, some general Old Testament references describe infertility as a judgment from God, though these appear to be national judgments for national disobedience. In other cases, the infertile couple is portrayed and even described as being righteous. In both Old Testament and New Testament examples of women with infertility—Sarah, Samson's mother, Hannah, Elizabeth—each woman plays a critical role in God's redemptive plan. Each is described favorably and blessed for her faith and prayer while enduring infertility.[1] In their cultures, not having an heir was a matter of great shame and was assumed (not always correctly) to be the result of God's judgment on the couple.

God certainly could use infertility or any other means to get the attention of His children. Yet, what we know about His character and the work of the Holy Spirit suggests that the believer under affliction would be made conscious of his or her rebellion and, therefore, be fully able to seek forgiveness and restoration. Restoration, however, would not guarantee pregnancy. Similarly, in the specific cases of extramarital sex leading to sterility from sexually transmitted disease complications or from complications following abortion, the act might have ongoing or permanent consequences. However, for the majority of cases, infertility would seem to be neither an issue of fault nor a consequence of divine judgment.

3. What is secondary infertility?

Generally, this term is applied to couples who have successfully given birth to one or more children and then are unable to conceive over one year's time. This segment of the population attracts little sympathy from those with primary infertility, but the emotional distress can be considerable. Simply having one child does not necessarily satisfy the desire for a family.

Because many of the parameters of fertility can change with time, couples with secondary infertility may require a broad spectrum of diagnostic testing and treatment options. Both the chronological age of the mother and the biological age of the ovary can contribute to the problem. Precise cyclical hormone production tends to decline with age. Endometriosis or occasionally tubal disease can develop. With divorce and remarriage so common today, people in fertile relationships with previous spouses may experience infertility in a new relationship.

4. What should I do if I am infertile?

If a couple finds that they meet the criteria for the diagnosis of infertility, either primary or secondary, what *can* be done and what *should* be done may be very different. For those with pronounced menstrual irregularity, waiting a year to be diagnosed as clinically infertile wastes valuable time. Infertility may stress a marriage in many ways—emotionally, financially, and spiritually. The couple must decide whether to seek treatment from medical personnel, seek support and counsel from trained professionals or friends, and/or keep the diagnosis private. Proceeding with medical evaluation or beginning the cascade of therapies requires careful deliberation.

Many decide not to pursue reproductive technologies or to limit their participation in them. Some people decide that having children now is not God's plan for their lives (see question 24). But for many, a clear diagnosis of infertility, if possible, can prove very helpful when contemplating treatment options or choosing to accept life without one's own biological children. Some settle the infertility question by looking into the adoption process. Adoption, however, can cost more than $20,000 and is by no means a sure thing (see questions 22 and 23).

Once a couple decides to pursue an infertility workup, selecting the appropriate physician or clinic can be crucial. Many physicians are knowledgeable and competent to investigate the cause of infertility, but there are those who have neither the interest nor the training to assist couples through this maze of testing and treatment plans. Most obstetrician-gynecologists can conduct the initial evaluation or refer couples to an appropriate fertility specialist. Family practitioners, internists, and urologists likewise can direct a couple to a physician who can provide ongoing care.

The initial phase of the diagnostic investigation is fairly straightforward and relatively inexpensive. It might include testing a man's semen for quality and quantity of sperm, evaluating ovulation and hormonal production in the woman, and scanning the pelvis with ultrasound to determine if the proper sequence of events in the ovary is occurring. Using simple techniques that require at-home temperature recording as well as urine tests often yield valuable information. For those inclined to begin the testing process, this series of evaluations can often uncover the general category of infertility and guide the physician's treatment plan. To decide what steps might improve the environment for conception and pregnancy, it may be necessary to conduct other tests to demonstrate that the fallopian tubes are normal and open: a laparoscopic evaluation (day surgery) of the pelvic organs in the female and further sophisticated immunologic (antibody problems) testing.

Since each of the procedures is complicated, couples must gain a basic understanding of the terminologies and procedures in order to make reasonable and ethical decisions. Each couple should discuss their values and beliefs with their health-care team before proceeding with even the simplest of interventions. Sometimes a simple course of antibiotics resolves infertility caused by infection, or the addition of thyroid hormone for an individual with low thyroid levels can correct the abnormality that was preventing pregnancy. The crucial first step is making the correct diagnosis so that the best treatment plan can be chosen, which may include no treatment at all. Most couples benefit from at least the basic evaluation before deciding whether or not to intervene; however, to make intervention decisions, more than medical and technical information is needed. People must also clarify their understanding of marriage and parenthood. As the answers to the next two questions demonstrate, the forms of assisted reproduction that are morally acceptable depend on such an understanding.

5. What is marriage?

Defining and understanding marriage within a culture remains central in formulating a consistent ethical position on reproductive issues. From a Christian perspective, marriage is an institution ordained by God, not originated by people. Consider first the biblical revelation concerning the marriage relationship before consulting the myriad of philosophical or psychological self-help books. Even for those unfamiliar or unconcerned with biblical teaching, the cultural aspects of marriage still have far-reaching effects in each society. For citizens of America, marriage involves a legal contract witnessed and validated by a justice of the peace, pastor, rabbi, or someone licensed by the state to conduct the legal ceremony. Most people recognize, by virtue of the high divorce rate in the United States, that legal implications and responsibilities exist within all marriages.

From a biblical perspective, marriage is a *covenant*, a binding agreement made before God. It is God who joins husband and wife together. Jesus said, "What . . . God has joined together, let no man separate" (Matt. 19:6).

According to God's instructions in Genesis, marriage involves two things: leaving and cleaving. "For this cause a man shall leave his father and mother and shall cleave to his wife; and they shall become one flesh" (Gen. 2:24). Thus, God creates a new family unit that takes priority over past family relationships. A one-flesh entity emerges that is new and unique. Recognizing the biblical one-flesh relationship is essential for constructing ethical guidelines. From a Christian worldview, the husband-wife bond is a one-of-a-kind relationship that carries with it many biblical instructions on how spouses are to live together (Gen. 2:18; Eph. 5:21–33; 1 Peter 3:1–7). The one-flesh imagery portrays God's design for marriage beyond physical oneness. Yet, it certainly anticipates physical intimacy as a central feature in marriage.

God joins a husband and wife together for intimacy of body, soul, and spirit.

From a Christian perspective, an understanding of God's design for marriage provides the basis for ethical decision making in the areas of sexuality and reproduction. Other worldviews likewise often hold a high view of marriage and family, and many consider marriage to serve as the moral platform for childbearing and child rearing.

6. What is parenthood?

Having considered the biblical origin and design of marriage, we can now address parenthood from a Christian perspective. Regardless of one's worldview, biological parenting consists of passing along genetic material from one generation to the next—a biological parent shares chromosomal makeup, or genes, with the offspring. Children are the fruit of the one-flesh relationship between husband and wife. Just as the two spouses become one, their gametes (sperm and egg) become one, resulting in a child for whom they are responsible.

Parenthood by definition encompasses both producing offspring and providing oversight. However, in this era of reproductive technology, the ability to mix and share gametes from donors and employ surrogates to carry pregnancies confuses and confounds definitions. Common use of the word *parent* involves more than the procreative act. It also signifies the time, effort, and love involved in rearing the children, regardless of the biological origins. For example, adoptive parents, stepparents, and foster parents represent vital roles that expand the understanding of parenthood and family. Single-parent families abound, and available technology opens the doors of parenthood to same-sex couples as well.

As we consider the complexities of biological origins in the remainder of these pages, great appreciation is expressed for the honorable role of the parent apart from the specific medical or procedural origin of the child. Men and women with widely divergent worldviews dedicate themselves to the character development of their children. We will consider in detail the ethics and theological concerns of donors, recipients, and surrogates.

Before proceeding, however, please consider one clarification that could spare you considerable frustration. Having children is more a privilege than a right. A couple who believes that having a child is a right may be blinded to anything except having a child and may make unwise reproductive decisions as a result. The potential physical harm that extended treatment may cause the woman, the financial expense that will result from multiple attempts at pregnancy, and the emotional toll that continued treatment may bring to bear on a marriage relationship can be avoided by couples who understand parenthood to be a privilege rather than a right.

An Old Testament woman who may provide some insight into this issue is Hannah, the beloved wife of Elkanah. The Scripture records that the "LORD had closed her womb." Today, we would say that Hannah was infertile (see question 2; according to 1 Sam. 1:5–7, her condition lasted "year after year"). It is important to note that Hannah did not know whether this "closure" was permanent or temporary. For this reason, she "prayed to the LORD and wept bitterly" (1 Sam. 1:10), hoping that her pleas would be heard and her infertility removed.

For Hannah, her prayers resulted in the opening of her womb and the subsequent birth of a son who was named Samuel, which means "name of God." His birth was a reminder to all that blessings come as a result of calling on the name of the Lord. Samuel was a gift given to a woman who petitioned the Lord. He was not a right; he was a privilege bestowed. This gift did not come cheaply for Hannah because she offered a condition on which her pregnancy was based: At the time of Samuel's weaning (possibly at age two or three), he was to be given to the Lord and then raised by Eli, the priest. Hannah's infertility was lifted in order to bear a child who would become a great prophet for the Lord (see also Sarah, Gen. 16:1–2; 21:2–7).

This wonderful story should cause all of us to reflect on the reasons we desire children. Nevertheless, regardless of *our* reasons, children are gifts from God, and God may allow infertility—even permanent infertility—for reasons that are unknown to us. There was no guarantee from the Lord that Hannah's womb would be opened. You can desire and pray for children—and take all available steps to have them—but the fruit of the womb is ultimately in the hand of God, not in technology. The *attitude* with which you approach parenthood and especially reproductive technology, initially determines whether or not any of the procedures described in this book are morally acceptable.

7. *What is sexual intercourse?*

In this age of phone sex, cybersex, and virtual-reality sex, we must reconsider even the definition of our sexuality. "Sexual intercourse" generally applies to the physical act of coitus where the penis is inserted into the vagina. Christians recognize two purposes for sexual intercourse: the unitive (for enjoyment and relationship building) and procreative (for having children). Christians differ over the exact connection between the two, and the implications this connection has for certain forms of contraception and assisted reproduction (see later questions). However, there is much that Christians hold in common. From a Christian perspective, sexuality is a wonderful gift from God intended for physical pleasure, emotional support, and spiritual unity.[2] Sexual intercourse is the natural means of reproduction, and the vast majority of humans result from natural conception. Medical advances, however, have permitted fertilization without intercourse. In fact, fertilization can now occur without the biological father and mother ever even meeting one another!

Sexuality has dimensions beyond reproduction and by design evokes powerful pleasurable sensations, including the release of endorphins with orgasm. Endorphins are potent, narcoticlike chemicals released within the brain that cause powerful euphoric sensations. Thus, there is a pleasure-driven urge that humans experience that makes intercourse a desirable activity. Sexual intercourse is intended to be an enjoyable experience between married individuals of opposite sexes. The Bible forbids premarital, extramarital, and homosexual intercourse. Jesus instructs in the Sermon on the Mount that sexual behavior that is pleasing to God goes beyond mere adherence to these guidelines and includes the thoughts and attitudes (Matt. 5:27–28). Jesus interprets the biblical commands about sexual purity to extend to controlling the mind.

Some worldviews that deny the Creator or reject ultimate human accountability may support wider sexual license. In the United States, premarital and extramarital sexual relations are common. The dramatic rise in cases of sexually transmitted disease and AIDS reflects this greater permissiveness.

8. What is an embryo?

Confusion over precise terminology can cause disagreements among individuals concerned with medical advances. Before considering the various procedures and options available in assisted reproduction, let us first clarify the terms. Technically, when a sperm and egg join together at conception, a zygote is formed. After one week, the zygote develops into an embryo. Then, after eight weeks, the embryo develops into a fetus. We will use the word *embryo* to refer to the first eight weeks of human development, except when an explicit distinction between the zygote and embryo is necessary (see question 15).

An embryo is a human being at an early stage of development. It is separate from the portion of the developing group of cells that become the placental or supportive tissue. After the sperm has penetrated the egg and when the chromosomes from the father and mother have aligned in the egg, fertilization has occurred. In a natural cycle, this event takes place in one of the fallopian tubes of the female. Many fertility clinics label the resultant living and growing tissue as "pre-embryo" because, as this developing cluster of cells grows, precisely which of the cells will become the baby and which will become the supportive structures is unknown. In fact, several of these early cells can die and the pregnancy can still proceed on the basis of the health of another cell. The earliest cells are believed to be "totipotential." That is, each cell can generate all the tissues necessary for a baby's development. No genetic material is added after the moment of fertilization. Each individual, from the moment of fertilization represents an individual of tremendous worth, created in the image of God. The psalmist describes God's creation of a child: "You wove me in my mother's womb" (Ps. 139:13). God views the embryo with the utmost of individual care and attention. The psalmist states that all of an individual's days, from fertilization to death are preordained "when as yet there was not one of them" (Ps. 139:16).

In approximately seven days, the growing collection of cells attaches to the wall of the uterus (womb), an event technically called "implantation." While people occasionally identify conception with implantation, conception ("the beginning") is better understood as referring to fertilization. Since all of life's genetic machinery that makes each individual unique originates with the fertilization event, any intervention after fertilization but before implantation that destroys the new human life is an abortion, not a contraceptive method. Use of the term *pre-embryo* should not desensitize us to the humanity and personhood of fertilized, dividing eggs that are created by assisted reproduction techniques. Some people would argue that we cannot abort (i.e., separate from the mother) what has not been attached. Yet, from the scientific, genetic point of view, life uniquely begins for a particular individual at the time of fertilization. The implantation event represents only the *nutritional connection*—the vital link between mother and developing infant—and not the starting point for that person.

Since embryos are tiny human beings, the destiny of frozen embryos (cryopreserved) is a serious concern. They are children whose parents must do all they can to sustain them and enable them to develop at the appropriate time. As this issue illustrates, making good decisions regarding the use of many available reproductive technologies hinges on understanding and communicating the unique vocabulary of reproduction precisely.

After the so-called embryonic stage, which lasts until approximately twelve weeks from the last menstrual period, the developing human is labeled a *fetus*. This term is utilized for the remainder of the pregnancy, regardless of the length of gestation. No dramatic events separate the embryonic period from the fetal period. It is simply a continuation of growth and development. Likewise, from the so-called pre-embryo stage to the embryonic stage, a gradual process of differentiation and maturation continues. Thus, it makes sense to have the same high regard for this unique individual human being from the very beginning of life when the genetic material (genome) is complete. What follows is just a part of growing up, growing older, and eventually leaving the womb for a more visible place of residence.

9. Should I consider the use of reproductive technologies?

The basic issue here is whether or not *any* medical interventions are moral. Some have promoted the idea that faith alone should be sufficient in all areas of life, including fertility. These individuals would deny medical intervention for any physical problem and rely only on prayers of faith. Christians, and others, more commonly believe that God created humanity and has permitted insight, though limited, into the complexities and functioning of the human body. Medical therapy is appropriate as long as no scriptural principle is violated. Most nontheistic worldviews applaud human insight and scientific discoveries and therefore allow experimentation and utilization of therapies for the common good. For example, antibiotics for infections, surgery for appendicitis, and chemotherapy for cancers are appropriate moral responses to human infirmity. Medical intervention is acceptable for couples facing infertility as long as other foundational principles are not violated. When people disagree over the use of particular reproductive technologies, it is usually because they disagree about fundamental principles such as the sanctity of embryonic life or the appropriateness of using technology to alter the natural way that fertilization takes place within the body.

As discussed in the previous question regarding the embryo, a widely held Christian conviction is that embryonic life is indeed sacred—that personhood begins at the moment of fertilization. Thus, cryopreservation (freezing) of embryos involves living persons in embryonic form. Discarding or destroying these embryos or using such embryos for research with or without parental consent or knowledge—unless the benefit to the embryo is greater than the risk—is ethically unacceptable. However, freezing sperm or eggs does not raise the same moral issues as freezing embryos, since individual human lives have not been created. Various other technologies similarly pose no moral dilemma to many who believe medical intervention to be an appropriate response to the problem of infertility. Legal, financial, and other pragmatic concerns must be addressed in each case, but these procedures can potentially be carried out with the highest respect for human life and dignity as long as the embryonic and other stages of human life are not devalued in the process.

Some Christians will question the appropriateness of any technology that alters the natural way fertilization takes place within the body—e.g., by enabling fertilization to take place in a petri dish in a laboratory. This position's appreciation of human life and God's design for procreation is laudable; however, such technological intervention need not cause a problem for Christians as long as the technology is making possible something that is in harmony with God's will (a married couple having children) *in a situation where the body is not functioning as God intends.*

10. *What about using fertility drugs?*

Depending on a couple's underlying medical condition, a myriad of medications can be used as fertility drugs because they enhance fertility. For a man with prostatic infection, a simple course of antibiotics might accurately be considered a fertility treatment. For a women with low thyroid, replacement thyroid hormone would represent a fertility drug. On the premise that medical intervention and drug therapy are moral options in general (see previous question), many treatment alternatives are acceptable and enhance fertility. In fact, any medication or surgical procedure that restores a patient to a more healthy, functional state would improve his or her fertility. The focus here, though, will be on drugs used to induce ovulation (egg production and/or release) or to improve sperm quality, quantity, or function.

For the woman who does not ovulate, introduction of ovulatory drugs has made pregnancy possible. Prior to the development of clomiphene citrate (Clomid, Serophene, and others) there was no effective therapy for women who did not ovulate; adoption was the only recourse. Clomiphene can stimulate ovulation in many women and does not have nearly as much risk of multiple pregnancies as do other drugs. The number of follicles (cystic structures within the ovary that harbor the maturing egg) can be monitored with ultrasound—multiple pregnancies can, therefore, usually be prevented. Specific messenger hormones, Follicle Stimulating Hormone (FSH) and Luteinizing Hormone (LH), are also available and constitute what most consider to be fertility drugs. These hormones directly stimulate the ovary—bypassing the built-in protective mechanisms—so that multiple eggs will mature. This can be the desired intent for egg harvesting, particularly in the high-tech procedures where growing ten to twenty eggs or more can facilitate the recovery of some good—healthy—mature eggs for fertilization.

Drug therapy for males has not been nearly as encouraging. But in those individuals where a problem with sperm has been corrected, the moral dilemma of producing multiple embryos does not apply. An egg will not normally be penetrated by more than one sperm, no matter how many are nearby.

11. What about artificial insemination?

By definition, this procedure involves putting the sperm into the vagina using a means other than the penis. The sperm that is used in this procedure comes from two sources: Sometimes it comes from the husband who has a problem such as a low sperm count or ejaculatory difficulties; other times it comes from a donor, perhaps via a donor sperm bank. Movies and comedians have dubbed this the "turkey baster" approach to conception because the doctor uses a sterile syringe for injecting the sperm. A small cap or diaphragm-like device suffices to "hold" the sperm in place for a while. Sometimes, though, the sperm requires special washing and then injection directly into the uterus instead of into the vagina. This whole procedure, intrauterine insemination (IUI), is carefully timed with the ovulatory cycle. Before the proliferation and spread of AIDS, hepatitis, and other sexually transmitted diseases (STDs), those electing to use donor sperm generally obtained fresh sperm from local donors. Although fresh sperm yields a somewhat higher pregnancy rate than frozen sperm, donor sperm is now typically frozen for six months after which time the donor is tested for AIDS. Once the sperm is deemed safe, it is released for use.

Artificial insemination is simple, relatively painless, and quite successful if used for the appropriate indications. It is an ethically acceptable option within the parameters of technological intervention already discussed (see question 9). However, is it ethical and legal to use *donor* sperm? After introducing the technology of *in vitro* fertilization in the next question, this question will be addressed.

12. *What about* in vitro *fertilization (IVF)?*

In vitro means "in glass" as opposed to within the living tissue system (*in vivo*). While commonly called test-tube fertilization, no test tubes are employed. Rather, flat culture dishes easily accessible to microscopes and micromanipulating instruments are used. IVF involves exposing the egg to the sperm in a carefully controlled, sterile environment. Therefore, fertilization occurs outside the human body rather than in the fallopian tubes as occurs naturally. The sperm can be obtained fresh or from thawed and prepared semen samples either from the husband or from a donor.

The physician obtains (recovers) the eggs, generally from the woman's hormonally hyperstimulated ovaries using a needle (transvaginal needle aspiration). Multiple ova can be harvested, and it is possible to freeze and later thaw some of them.

Fertilization normally occurs without any special manipulation. However, in the case of older eggs or a markedly diminished sperm count, special procedures can be instituted to increase the chances of fertilization (see question 16 on intracytoplasmic sperm injection [ICSI] for a description of these techniques).

Those considering *in vitro* fertilization will want to know the success rates of various clinics. Since success should mean actually having a baby, people must specifically ask for the live birth rate as opposed to the fertilization rate. The live birth rates at most clinics range from 20 percent to 40 percent. One must bear in mind that some of the best clinics may have lower success rates because they will treat older patients or patients with multiple medical complications.

Once fertilization has occurred outside the body, a

particular number of cell divisions will take place over a period of hours before the growing embryos (or pre-embryos as some call them) are transferred into the uterus of the woman carrying the pregnancy. This process is called embryo transfer (ET). This is an important term in that the same designation is used in animal husbandry for the transfer of an embryo from within the womb of one animal to the womb of a second, surrogate animal. Some confuse the procedure in humans with the very different technique in animals. In reproductive clinics, embryo transfer is the procedure of removing the group of dividing cells from the culture dish in the laboratory and inserting them into the mother. Generally this is a relatively painless, fairly quick procedure with little or no anesthesia needed.

When a husband's sperm and a wife's egg are used, IVF, in effect, merely bypasses the fallopian tubes. Thus, in the case of tubal damage or disease or for some with undiagnosed infertility, this procedure provides an avenue for the husband and wife to contribute their own genetic material and become biological parents. Likewise, IVF can enable men with very low sperm counts to biologically father their own offspring.

As a cure for infertility, IVF fits within the ethical parameters for technological intervention considered earlier (see question 9). Each embryo *can* be reverenced and treated with dignity. Nothing about the mechanics of the procedure makes it inherently unethical for those who believe medical intervention to be moral unless one holds the position that the physical act of intercourse (unitive purpose) cannot be even temporarily separated from procreation (Vatican's position). Even then, special condoms with tiny perforations are available for Roman Catholics to comply, at least in part, with the Vatican's position by allowing at least the chance of pregnancy while collecting sperm in the condom during intercourse.

That IVF is an option to consider does not mean that it is right for every infertile couple that might be helped by it. IVF is time consuming, expensive, and not without some risk from drug therapy and invasive procedures, such as needle retrieval of the eggs and placement of the embryos into the vagina and through the cervix. This risk may be somewhat diminished as the procedure for freezing and thawing eggs becomes more efficient with a decreasing rate of loss. Thus, freezing and storing eggs will increase availability and decrease cost.

Moreover, there are some significant choices to make regarding how IVF is done that can alter the ethical acceptability of the procedure. These decisions should be addressed with a fertility specialist who will respect and support your theological and philosophical views. Limits can and should be placed on the number of eggs fertilized, the number of embryos reimplanted, and the fate of frozen embryos (if this avenue is taken). In light of the special importance of embryonic life, you will want to avoid selective reduction after implantation, i.e., the destruction of extra embryos to enhance the survivability of the remaining embryos. It is similarly unacceptable to transfer so many embryos into the uterus that the likelihood of all the embryos implanting is significantly diminished. One good approach is to transfer two or three. Whether or not some of the embryos produced are to be frozen, the total number of eggs fertilized should *not* be higher than the number of children you are willing to have.

It is essential for couples to understand the specific procedures, possibilities, risks, benefits, and safeguards before considering the rightness or wrongness of IVF for them. The assumption to this point has been that the couple will be using the husband's sperm and the wife's eggs. We turn next to the question of using donor sperm or eggs.

13. Is it okay for me to use a donor's egg or sperm to conceive a child?

What would you do if your medical circumstances required the use of donor gametes? Or what would you add to your family's gene pool if you had the opportunity? What are the ethical issues involved in bringing a third reproductive party, usually anonymous, into a marriage relationship?

Large donor-sperm programs screen donors well for sexually transmittable diseases and have information about the donor's blood type, physical features, and genetic background. Having this knowledge can relieve some of the anxiety concerning medical risks. But some have objected to the use of donor gametes on the grounds that some sort of adultery is actually committed in the process. They have argued that despite the absence of physical contact, donor insemination still violates the sanctity of marriage; however, everything that violates the sanctity of marriage is not adultery. It is better to reserve the word *adultery* for sexual relationships, whether actual or desired, that violate the marriage union.

Opinions within the Christian community diverge based on many factors, including how individuals interpret the Old Testament story of Onan and the "levirate marriage." The Bible (Gen. 38) outlines a circumstance in which a man died childless and his brother was obligated to provide offspring to the widow. Onan had a sexual relationship with his brother's widow, but he withdrew, "spilling his seed on the ground." God struck him dead for his disobedience.

People draw varying conclusions and applications from this interesting passage. In this narrow circumstance, producing offspring takes an important precedence over sexuality bounded exclusively by traditional marriage. However, even this arrangement—a levirate marriage (from the Latin *levir*, "brother-in-law")—is a *marriage*. The widow becomes a (perhaps second) wife to the man. The prohibition against premarital or extramarital sex is not suspended here; rather, the structure of the family is adapted to the special needs of early Israel.[3]

This principle has been invoked to support donor insemination for the infertile male. However, *not just any male would do* in the patriarchal Jewish community of the Old Testament. A brother, a descendant of the same tribe, was required. Israel, as a people of God, was at an early stage of its existence in which the tribal/clan/family system was extremely important and still in the process of being established. Thus, there are significant differences between this exceptional circumstance in Scripture and the typical situation in which the use of donor sperm is contemplated today. Biblical instances where donor eggs are used provide even less support. For example, when Abraham had a child with his servant Hagar— unfortunately with his wife's blessing—it is portrayed as contrary to God's will (Gen. 16; see question 18 on surrogate motherhood).

As to the issue of donor eggs, availability and

expense become another issue. The prospective egg donor must be hormonally synchronized with the recipient mother using powerful ovary-stimulating medications to mature multiple eggs for harvesting. This harvesting of the donor's eggs is accomplished using transvaginal ultrasound and a guided needle through the vagina (previously, laparoscopy was required to recover the eggs, generating considerable expense and risks involved in general anesthesia and surgical procedures). Once harvested, the eggs are used almost immediately, since the recipient mother is precisely at the right stage of her cycle to receive the fertilized eggs. As freezing and thawing eggs continues to become more efficient (see previous question), it will become a more attractive alternative. Also on the horizon is the possibility of harvesting ovaries from aborted fetuses and maturing the eggs in the laboratory for future donation. One of the many problems with this arrangement is that the biological mother cannot fulfill her appropriate responsibility to care for her children; she herself has never been born.

The attractiveness of using donor gametes is understandable. Donor sperm use has certain advantages, including decreased cost when compared to adoption or high-tech procedures. It also provides safe donors, presumably well screened for genetic factors and medical history. Couples may well appreciate that the child will be biologically related to at least one parent and that the mother can carry the child and control the prenatal environment. As for egg donation, screening the candidates can decrease some genetic problems. Moreover, the child will carry the genetics of the husband, and often the recipient mother will carry the child, thereby emotionally connecting with the child through gestation.

However, the emotional considerations involved in the use of donor gametes are complex. Emotional stress may develop within the marriage when one of the partners is not biologically connected to the child, even though the procedure was undertaken with full knowledge and consent. In a very real (biological-genetic) sense, one of the partners has had a child together with someone other than their spouse, and that facet can foster an emotional interest in the donor (even if anonymous). There is also a greater risk that a parent who has no genetic link to the child may, under pressure, take less responsibility for the child than will the parent with the genetic link.

The more basic teaching of Scripture is the one-flesh principle, based on the declaration in Genesis that when a man leaves his family and takes a wife the two become one flesh. This principle, as the authors here understand it, allows reproductive technology that enables a husband and wife to produce offspring by assisted means but would exclude the use of donor sperm or eggs being joined with the gametes of the husband or wife.

14. What about gamete intrafallopian transfer (GIFT)?

The word *gamete* refers to the male or female cell (sperm or egg), each of which contains half the number of chromosomes typically present in a body cell. When a sperm and egg join together, a new and complete set of chromosomes (genome, or genetic code) is created for the new embryo and for every cell that will develop during pregnancy and beyond.

The technique for GIFT involves laparoscopy, a surgical procedure requiring general anesthesia. This procedure is commonly called band-aid surgery because the incisions are quite small, and the patient is discharged the same day from the hospital or clinic. During this procedure, the operating surgeon can see the organs of the pelvis by inserting a tiny video camera that allows the procedure to be displayed on a video monitor. The procedure is timed precisely to coincide with egg ripening, which is generally controlled by hormonal stimulation so as to not miss the egg release. When one or more preovulatory follicles come into view, the eggs (one per follicle) are aspirated (i.e., to draw or remove by suction) with a needle (similar to another technique used for harvesting eggs through the vagina using ultrasound to guide the needle). Each egg is examined immediately in an adjacent laboratory and graded for quality, then reloaded into a special syringe. The sperm specimen is specially prepared to increase the percentage of healthy sperm. The specialist loads the sperm into the same syringe with at least one egg. The operating surgeon transfers this material gently into the fallopian tube with the aid of the same tiny camera. The fallopian tube is the precise location where fertilization normally takes place. In fact, a chemical from tubal-lining cells seems to enhance the ability of the embryo to implant into the wall of the uterus. Some IVF clinics are trying to duplicate this enhancing factor during those hours before reimplantation.

With GIFT, fertilization occurs in the fallopian tube, if it occurs at all. There is an element of uncertainty, but with normal tubes, a mature egg, and an adequate sperm specimen, pregnancy rates are good. Cost is significant because of the surgical procedure involved and the reoperation required for each cycle until fertilization and conception occur. Physicians can now access the fallopian tubes with tiny scopes through the vagina and cervix. One day physicians may be able to eliminate the laparoscopy from the procedure and perform GIFT in an office setting.

To be sure, it is medically possible to place within the syringe sperm and eggs from non-related donors and transfer the mix into the wife for the pregnancy, producing a child without genetic relation to the husband or wife. However, physicians can perform GIFT using a husband's and wife's gametes and do so without jeopardizing any embryos. Accordingly, the procedure can fit within the moral guidelines laid out in questions 9, 13, and 18. For some people, GIFT is even less objectionable than IVF, since fertilization takes place naturally in the normal bodily location and manner. For the treatment of male infertility, and occasionally for infertility without a discernible cause, GIFT has an acceptable live birth rate. There are no extra embryos or frozen embryos to consider, and absolute control of the number of eggs transferred gives the couple a sense of acting within conscience.

15. What about zygote intrafallopian transfer (ZIFT)?

A zygote is the cell formed by the joining of the gametes (sperm and egg). The zygote stage is the first phase of human development from fertilization up through the first week of gestation. From the zygote come all the cells that make up a person and all the supportive structures of pregnancy (placenta, cord, amniotic membranes, and so forth). The zygote has the full genetic code, half from the sperm and half from the egg. Occasionally, with identical twinning and cloning (to be discussed later), this genetic material duplicates in another individual.

The procedure for ZIFT is similar to GIFT, including the hormonal preparation of the woman and egg harvest (generally by ultrasound guided-needle retrieval) at the same time that the preparation of the sperm specimen takes place. Then the egg is exposed to the sperm outside the mother's body in a petri dish where fertilization occurs. Once the sperm has penetrated the egg and the visible microscopic changes are noted, the physician places the zygote, by laparoscopy, into the fallopian tube of the recipient mother. In a natural pregnancy, the zygote normally develops in the fallopian tube; thus, this procedure attempts to duplicate the natural events as much as possible in situations where the more controlled environment of the lab is necessary to achieve fertilization.

The couple can avoid ethical concerns over cryopreservation or extra embryos by controlling the number of zygotes formed. This allows the procedure to be accomplished with high respect for the life and dignity of each zygote that develops. As long as the use of donor gametes is avoided (see question 13) and the cautions regarding the use of a surrogate mother are heeded (see question 18), this technology may fall within the guidelines for an ethically acceptable medical intervention (see question 9). Nevertheless, because the use of this technology, like IVF, removes fertilization from its natural location in the body (in a fallopian tube) and involves many pragmatic costs, people should resort to it only when it is the least costly option with a reasonable likelihood of success.

16. What about intracytoplasmic sperm injection (ICSI) and related options?

By way of example and for the purpose of clarification only, consider the chicken egg. Its key structures include an easily recognizable shell, an egg white, and a yolk. The human egg is too small to see without the aid of a microscope, but it has these similar components: a so-called shell, material called cytoplasm (like the egg white), and a nucleus (like a yolk). While the human egg shell is not hard like the chicken egg, it is thicker than the cytoplasm it contains. As the woman ages, her remaining eggs usually have even tougher shells.

ICSI. The ICSI procedure involves the injection of a *single* human sperm into a human egg by piercing the shell with a specially prepared microscopic needle (a "micromanipulative" procedure). The eggs are retrieved as previously described in the section on GIFT. Ordinarily the eggs are retrieved from the wife who will be the biological mother. However, the use of donor eggs and, as technology permits, thawed eggs is technologically feasible. The sperm is obtained from the male (often, but not necessarily by masturbation), and the specimen is prepared. The embryologist selects and loads a single normal-appearing sperm into the microinjecting apparatus. The source of the sperm used in this procedure is sometimes the husband and sometimes a donor.

Once the sperm is loaded into the microneedle, the egg is stabilized under the microscope and the shell is pierced with the needle. The sperm is then injected directly into the cytoplasm (like the egg white). From this point, the chromosomes of the sperm must align with the chromosomes of the egg. In a wonderfully complex and poorly understood series of events, the egg *knows* that penetration has occurred and the chromosomes of the egg, which are located in the nucleus (like the yolk), unravel and align with the male's chromosomes. Only then has a unique individual, with the complete chromosomal complement necessary for life and growth, emerged.

Assisted Hatching. Another micromanipulative technique related to ICSI is assisted hatching. With the increasing age of the egg, there may be problems with sperm penetration. A woman is born with all the eggs she will ever have, though they are in an immature state. Generally, the most hormone-responsive eggs ovulate first, in early life. Thus, older women wishing to conceive may have more difficulty with fertilization and hatching. In an effort to assist these women, the shell of the egg may be scored or scratched to create a weakened point that will permit the egg to hatch. Most people have seen a tiny chick break through the shell and, over the course of minutes, achieve freedom from the confines of the hard chicken eggshell. In humans, following fertilization, the cell begins to divide and expand within the confines of the shell and, therefore, needs to break through as cell number and size increases. If the human egg shell proves too difficult to break or hatch, the embryo will die. Microscopically assisting this process by scratching through a part of the shell during the micromanipulation allows some increased success. Hatching raises no significant additional moral issues not raised by ICSI itself.

ROSNI. In cases of male infertility when no mature sperm are produced or delivered, physicians may use round spermatic nuclear injection (ROSNI). It is rarely needed, but certain males benefit from ROSNI. It is helpful for men who lack or have total blockage of the vas deferens (the duct that carries the spermatozoa from the testis). Sperm is produced in the testicles but does not mature properly or cannot be ejaculated normally. The physician obtains immature sperm by needle aspiration of the epididymis (a tubular structure attached to the back of the testicle where spermatozoa is stored and matures before ejaculation) or of the testicle itself. These sperm have not matured but can be injected into the cytoplasm of the egg using a micromanipulative procedure, much as described in actual ICSI. Physicians recommend this procedure for the husband who has essentially no chance of producing a biological child without high-tech assistance. The relevant ethical issues are essentially those related to ICSI.

The moral issues involving ICSI are not new. The technology and ability to place a single sperm within a single egg represents a major breakthrough from the standpoint of treating male infertility. No longer are huge numbers of normal sperm necessary to achieve a pregnancy. Men with far lower sperm counts now have a reasonable chance of fathering a child. The temptation to use a donor with a higher sperm count is thereby lessened. ICSI may also eliminate a second reason why some people use donor sperm. At present, donor sperm can be used to avoid certain hereditary diseases. Future insight into the genetics of sperm may allow genetic testing and specific selection to avoid passing on certain abnormalities contained in the genetic code of only some of the husband's sperm. Even if all of the husband's sperm are affected, future genetic therapy techniques may well make it possible to correct a genetic deficiency in a sperm before employing ICSI.

Regardless of the state of genetic technology, though, the use of donor gametes is not ethically acceptable (see question 13; see also question 18 regarding the use of surrogate mothers). However, within the marriage union, ICSI is a potentially justifiable medical intervention on the same grounds as ZIFT and IVF (see question 9). In fact, it may be ethically preferable. With ICSI, physicians have absolute control of the number of embryos replaced, so there are no worries about unintended multiple pregnancies, cryopreservation, or the selective reduction of embryos.

17. *What are the legal issues with reproductive technologies?*

Initially, couples may wonder if their insurance provides coverage for infertility treatments. Only a few states require insurers to do so. For specific information on insurance coverage, contact the InterNational Council on Infertility Information Dissemination, P.O. Box 6836, Arlington, VA 22206 (http://www.inciid.org).

There are a number of other potentially thorny legal questions surrounding the use of reproductive technology, including: (1) What is the legal identity of the offspring? (2) Who may perform the assisted reproduction? (3) What type of consent is required? (4) What are the parameters for donor selection? and (5) What is the basis for potential liability? The law has yet to address these fully.

For couples considering assisted reproductive techniques using their own sperm and egg to impregnate the wife, key legal concerns involve *in vitro* production of multiple embryos and decisions about disposing of cryopreserved (frozen) embryos. Clinics require detailed planning in the event of divorce, death of one partner, or abandonment of stored embryos. What rights are to be ascribed to frozen progeny? How will they be handled in custody matters or financial responsibility? How will the clinic decide to dispose of excess, unwanted, or abandoned embryos? What will the couple do if they successfully complete their pregnancies but have multiple embryos still frozen?

When assisted reproduction techniques employ third-party gametes, whether donor sperm or eggs, additional concerns surface. In these situations, the most common legal questions concern adultery; legitimacy of the child; and the related problems of child support, custody, and inheritance. Although the child is technically illegitimate because the biological parents were not married to each other, most jurisdictions will consider the child legitimate if born during the marriage or within ten months of dissolution by death or divorce. States with statutes that directly address the question consider the child to be legitimate if the husband consented to the insemination. Challenges are generally raised only when the marriage breaks up.

Donor sperm has a long history, and most states do not hold the donor legally responsible for the offspring. However, some offspring of donor insemination are seeking to uncover the identity of their biological parent. Paid sperm donors have historically had no personal contact with their offspring or financial responsibility for them. The situation with the egg donor seems more complex. The retrieval of eggs often involves drug therapy and medical intervention or laparoscopic surgery. This adds risk and expense for the donor and may interfere with anonymity. Recent advances in freeze-thaw technique with ova (eggs) increases the likelihood that eggs can be stored in large numbers for use long after retrieval.

In fact, some investigators are pursuing the possibility of harvesting ovaries from aborted fetuses with the goal of maturing these eggs for later use in an egg donation program. While this prospect might generate a huge resource of eggs, the possibility exists for a child to have a genetic mother who never lived outside the womb. The ability to obtain sperm posthumously or to bank sperm from a man with terminal illness has already raised the issue of legal responsibility, rights, and inheritance claims for an individual conceived after the death of the biological father.

Parental informed consent is a necessary requirement whenever conception involves a donor's sperm or egg. The spouse whose gametes are *not* going to be used must give written and informed consent to the procedure to preclude a later claim of adultery or disavowal of parental responsibility. Even when parental consent is obtained, legal complications may follow. In fact, there are a variety of situations in which donors or parents may initiate law suits. A semen donor may bring suit to claim paternity, to obtain visitation rights, or to gain access to the mother's estate (for the benefit of the child) if the child is a minor. Parents might sue for "wrongful birth," in the event that a child is handicapped but would not have been born had the physician adequately advised the parents about prenatal testing. The inherent assumption is that the couple would abort any "unsatisfactory" fetus rather than bring the child to term.

Physicians are at legal risk for other reasons as well. The assisting physician may face liability for negligence, for example, in screening the donor. Women have contracted infections from contaminated semen. Physicians may be less apt to do genetic screening, but liability may arise if the child is born with a hereditary disease (or, as has happened, is a child of a different race than the mother).

Not surprisingly, the uses of reproductive technologies that are least justifiable ethically often turn out to be more problematic legally. But some potentially ethical uses also entail legal risks that may render pursuing them unwise. In any case, whatever legal risks are involved should be known and taken into consideration.

18. What about surrogate motherhood?

People sometimes consider the use of a surrogate mother in circumstances in which the wife cannot carry a pregnancy due to age, physical abnormality, illness, bodily injury, or immunologic problems (antibody reactions to pregnancy). In many instances the surrogate provides not only the host uterus or womb where the infant will grow but the egg as well (traditional surrogacy); however, this is not necessarily so. With the advent of the previously described IVF, ICSI, and other micro-manipulative techniques, it is possible for the surrogate to have no biological genetic connection with the child she is carrying (gestational surrogacy). In these instances, the surrogate serves as a living incubator for the offspring of others. As such, the relationship can be strictly financial or more altruistic with a family member or friend carrying the pregnancy as an act of love. While these situations can be very complicated legally (see question 19), the biology is quite simple. Gestational surrogacy has as its goal new life. For women who by reason of surgery or immune problems cannot carry a pregnancy, the so-called good goal of one's own genetic offspring is achieved.

Nevertheless, surrogacy is ethically unacceptable in two circumstances. The first concerns surrogacy that is for hire (commercial surrogacy). It is morally unacceptable to rent a womb for the purpose of having a child. The financial contract involves the purchase of a human being and, therefore, becomes a form of ownership of one person over another. Like the selling of any organs, the use of the womb as an organ for hire commercializes what should never be bought or sold. It is oppressive particularly for impoverished women who can be coerced financially into making their wombs available.

The second circumstance under which surrogacy must be deemed unethical concerns the use of a donor egg and/or sperm (see question 13), especially if one of these is joined with an egg or sperm from one of the spouses to create a child. Admittedly, the egg and the sperm may be fertilized *in vitro* (in a petri dish) or the surrogate may be artificially inseminated with the husband's sperm (as in traditional surrogacy); thus avoiding adultery in the traditional sense that this term signifies two people having a sexual relationship. Nevertheless, the crucial ethical flaw here is that the child created is not a product of the marriage union. To say that the child is, at least, a part of *us* is incorrect. The marriage union is the joining of two individuals into one flesh. A child whom either spouse produces apart from the other is not of this one-flesh union and, therefore, cannot be claimed as a product of the union. The child would be the product of *another union* that is not sanctioned by the marriage vows and commitment. The use of donor gametes takes technology outside of the bounds of marriage to create what the union itself is unable to create.

Is surrogacy morally acceptable if the gametes (egg and sperm) that are joined *in vitro* originate from the spouses of a marriage union? To be considered moral, surrogacy must avoid the problems of commercial surrogacy and donor gametes just discussed. Moreover, it must not be unwise in light of all the legal and pragmatic considerations involved. Regarding the first test, in situations where IVF is moral (see question 12) and the mother cannot carry a fetus, surrogacy provides a potentially moral means to enable the embryo to survive. If IVF is seen as the bypass of nonworking fallopian tubes, then surrogacy can be viewed as the bypass of the nonfunctional tubes and uterus. However, for such surrogacy to be morally acceptable, a surrogate must *volunteer her womb* without her imposing any conditions beyond receiving proper medical attention throughout the pregnancy.

We should commend, not condemn, a woman who, for the love of life, volunteers her womb to save a frozen embryo chosen for destruction. Moreover, we accept and laud a person who donates a lung or a kidney to save the life of a loved one. We should also laud the willingness of a woman who, without desire for personal gain, donates the use of her womb so that a couple she loves can *produce a child from their marital union*. If her motive is pure, the donation of her womb is a sacrificial act of love. The difference between the donation of a lung or kidney and that of a womb is that the woman who donates her womb gets the use of her organ back.

Yet, even in those situations where surrogacy is not inherently immoral, it may still not be the right course of action for a variety of legal and pragmatic considerations. The legal considerations will be addressed in the next question. The pragmatic concerns are not just financial but also profoundly emotional. Surrogacy requires a woman to break off, or at least radically alter, the relationship she has been developing with the child in her womb for nine months. Some surrogates cannot bring themselves to end this relationship, despite their best intentions at the outset, and so refuse to give up the baby at birth. This problem may be less likely to occur if the surrogate is a family member, so such an arrangement is usually preferable.

Nevertheless, any surrogacy arrangement brings a third party into the picture—thereby potentially distancing the mother from the child emotionally. It also becomes easier for one or both parents to disavow responsibility for the child in the surrogate's womb if they learn that the child has some disability (perhaps due to some unhealthy behavior by the surrogate).

Emotional difficulties only escalate in traditional surrogacy where the child is the genetic union, not of the husband and wife, but of the husband and surrogate. Improper emotional ties easily develop between the husband and surrogate—at least in the mind of the wife. A biblical story closest to resembling traditional surrogacy is the Old Testament account of Abraham and Sarah's use of a surrogate, Hagar, to enable Abraham to have genetic offspring (Gen. 16). Not only is it evident from the text that this step was a product of desperation rather than God's direction, but the result was the conflict between Sarah and Hagar that continued through their children (Isaac versus Ishmael) to the present day.

19. What legal issues pertain to surrogacy?

This question is enormously complex because the answer varies so widely from state to state. In fact, surrogacy is not legal in some states. Other states have laws that recognize surrogacy, while many others have taken a rather neutral approach. Thus, this brief treatment should not be considered legal advice in this rapidly changing field.

Traditional or "straight" surrogacy involves fertilizing the surrogate's egg with the sperm of the husband using artificial-insemination techniques. In this situation, the "gestational mother" (the woman carrying the pregnancy) is also the biological, genetic mother. The "intended" mother, or wife of the husband donating the sperm, has no genetic connection with the child and does not participate in the pregnancy. In states permitting such surrogate arrangements, the intended mother must file for legal adoption after the birth of the infant since the birth mother is usually assumed to be the legal mother. On the other hand, so-called "host" or gestational surrogacy involves the gestational mother's womb but not her egg. Thus, the gestational mother in this instance carries no genetic link—only the pregnancy link. Nevertheless, a legal-adoption procedure may well still be required for the intended mother.

Surrogacy is increasingly common. Some claim that as many as fifteen thousand surrogate births have been contracted. Of these, about a dozen have ended up in litigation. Many people will remember "Baby M" and Mary Beth Whitehead, her surrogate mother who changed her mind about signing over her daughter to William Stern—the sperm donor—and his wife. Although Ms. Whitehead ultimately lost custody of the child, the New Jersey Supreme Court declared surrogate contracts unenforceable.

These cases revolve around the surrogate mother's refusal to relinquish her parental rights and her baby, either before or shortly after birth. The legal issues may be decided under (1) contract law, (2) laws prohibiting black-market babies, (3) adoption laws prohibiting payments for bearing a child (the wife must adopt the baby, since she is not biologically related to the child), (4) family law regarding the biological (and contracting) father's petition for custody, or (5) rights and obligations of sperm donors.

The strangest twist in determining legal parentage involves the case of Jaycee Buzzanca, who for a time was legally "parentless." She was conceived by anonymous donor egg and sperm and born in 1995 to a surrogate mother hired by John and Luanne Buzzanca. The surrogate mother relinquished all her parental rights. The Buzzancas separated before the baby was born, so two-year-old Jaycee resides with Luanne. John refused to pay child support and declared he was not the father. The trial court declared that Jaycee has *no* parents and is not entitled to child support. The appellate court recently ruled that John Buzzanca is the legal father and ordered him to pay child support.[4]

In light of the possible combinations of a donor's egg, a donor's sperm, a husband's sperm, a wife's egg, and a surrogate mother being involved, the social and legal complexity of surrogacy is enormous. Think about the couple who has already obtained a donor egg, fertilized it *in vitro* with donor sperm, and implanted an embryo in a surrogate uterus. Each of the individuals involved—the two intended parents, the two donors, the surrogate, and even the spouse of the surrogate—may have legal claim to the resulting infant.

Some states are considered "surrogate friendly" because there are currently no statutes prohibiting or regulating the practice. Some states have legislation pending that might dramatically impact the validity of surrogacy contracts. These complicated documents spell out the intentions of the parties involved with the surrogate mother relinquishing parental rights to the child before fertilization. While these contracts can be meticulously drafted, it is uncertain how legally binding they are. Again, the law assumes that the woman who gives birth is legally the mother. Some test cases have seen the contracts thrown out because a woman cannot relinquish parental rights to a child not yet conceived. The legal rights of the surrogate's husband are not yet clearly defined. At times, the surrogate may fear that the intended parents will change their minds, leaving her with the child. Other surrogates change their minds and sue for custody of the baby. Even the names on the birth certificate can be challenged.

To further complicate matters, some states have declared that receiving a fee beyond the medical expenses (which is customary in surrogate situations) is illegal. This complication may arise when the intended parents seek to file formal adoption papers. Often they will be asked whether a fee was paid to the birth mother to facilitate adoption. Even the payment of normal medical fees may violate the law.

As of this writing, nineteen states have directly addressed surrogacy. Five states (Arizona, Michigan, New York, Utah, and Washington) plus the District of Columbia, criminalize surrogacy. However, the laws are often not enforced. An additional six states (Arkansas, Florida, Nevada, New Hampshire, North Dakota, and Virginia) permit surrogate arrangements, although three of them prohibit surrogate programs (Florida, New Hampshire, and Virginia). Contracts for surrogacy are not enforceable in five states (Indiana, Kentucky, Louisiana, Nebraska, and New Jersey). The contracting couple is at risk of losing their investment if the surrogate mother changes her mind about relinquishing the baby.

West Virginia, considered to be surrogate friendly, has an exception in its law prohibiting the "purchase or sale" of a child or the payment for consent to adopt. This exception allows for "fees and expenses included in any agreement" in which the woman consents to being a surrogate mother. Thus, West Virginia has recognized surrogacy as a legal arrangement. Other states have recognized the rights of genetic parentage in those rare cases of host surrogacy where the gestational mother sued for custody.

Other legal complications arise in cases of disability, divorce, or death. Parties may end up in court if the child is born with a disability and none of the parties involved wants to accept parental responsibility. When the intended parents divorce or in the event of the death of one of the intended parents, there is no genetic link between either intended parent and the offspring if donor gametes have been used. Thus, the legal responsibility in the event of divorce or death reverts to the intent outlined in the contract. But, as noted, these contracts may not be legally binding in some states.

The agency making the surrogacy arrangements could be sued for malpractice if it does not adequately screen the surrogate mother or donor parents. In one case, the surrogate mother contracted a virus from the donor father. In another, the surrogate mother refused to remain celibate and delivered a child fathered by her boyfriend. The couple had made payments to her for four months before the paternity of the child was determined.

The complicated legal issues are very real and persons considering surrogacy must seek qualified local legal expertise to understand all that is at stake legally.

20. Should I have my embryo genetically tested?

Prenatal testing represents a rapidly expanding area of obstetrical care. Physicians of an earlier era relied on the rate of uterine growth, the activity of the child, and a heartbeat detectable after five months to monitor the well-being of a fetus. Little else was discernible until birth. Today, physicians can perform amniocentesis (i.e., test the amniotic fluid) to detect numerous conditions. Using precise ultrasound equipment, they can observe much of the developmental processes. Tests on the amniotic fluid, examining the placental tissue by chorionic villus sampling and/or fetal blood reveal certain genetic and metabolic information. Certain hereditary disorders can be diagnosed, but few effective treatments are currently available. Sometimes this information is used to recommend abortion, particularly the procedures that diagnose conditions early in the pregnancy.

In this era of high-tech assisted reproduction, sperm and egg can meet *in vitro,* and the first cell division can take place outside the body. It is now possible to test one of the cells of the developing cluster and find helpful information before implantation. The Human Genome Project, currently mapping the entire genetic code in human beings, will eventually make it possible to predict from the earliest stage of life the certainty or likelihood that someone will develop a particular problem or abnormality.

What benefit does obtaining this information produce? What risk does genetic screening and testing carry for the embryo? Each of the invasive procedures carries risk. Amniocentesis and chorionic villus sampling can cause a normal pregnancy to abort. While this risk is quite low (approximately one in one thousand pregnancies with sonographically directed needle placement for amniocentesis, and slightly higher for the chorionic villus sampling), the risk is real. Freezing and thawing embryos likewise entails an appreciable, though decreasing, risk to the embryo. How much risk is acceptable?

A key question to ask about any of these invasive procedures is: How will any information obtained from it benefit the embryo? The experience of Nazi Germany taught us something. To guard against experimentation that would be harmful to the subjects, the Nuremberg Code was formulated and affirmed internationally.[5] It specifies that only experimentation potentially beneficial to the subject is ethical, unless the subject's informed consent can be obtained. Since the embryo's consent cannot be obtained, genetic testing *must be for the benefit of the embryo*, not for the purpose of abortion because the embryo has the full moral status of a person (see question 8).

For those who think that true humanity does not begin with fertilization, but with implantation, the first brain waves, the initial heart beat, or at some other milestone, the situation is very different. If the embryo is not a unique human life, then it follows that no *person* is at risk in embryonic testing. Thus, any experimentation deemed useful to society or any tests that might help a woman make a decision in favor of abortion can be carried out without moral constraints.

However, for those holding to the personhood of the embryo from the moment of fertilization, embryonic testing would need to have a benefit to the embryo exceeding the risk. Certain hereditary problems could be diagnosed, and as gene therapies develop, the potential exists for meaningful intervention at the embryonic stage. This is a worthy goal, but we must get there by ethical means. Where possible, information and technical expertise should be gained through experimentation *on cellular structures* rather than human embryos. However, if human embryos must be involved, they themselves must stand to benefit. With these stipulations, we maintain respect for the dignity of human life even in embryonic form.

21. *What about human cloning?*

Cloning is not a reproductive option presently available to couples; but, someday it may be. Thus, it warrants some attention here.

Publicity surrounding the reported production of the sheep clone, Dolly, has spurred a heated public debate. In January, 1998, President Clinton publicly reaffirmed his rejection of human cloning—a practice referred to as "playing God." In the same month, a Chicago physician pledged to begin offering human cloning to the public relatively soon, and nineteen European nations meeting in Paris, France, signed an agreement banning human cloning.

Animal husbandry experimentation has yielded considerable insight into twinning and genetic research. But Dolly's case goes beyond mere twinning. Reports maintain that researchers for the first time successfully cloned an animal using a nonreproductive cell (i.e., not a sperm or egg) from an adult. To do this, they extracted the genetic material from the cell by removing the cell's nucleus. This nucleus was then inserted into an egg whose own nucleus had been removed. Stimulated to divide by the application of electrical energy, this egg had the same complete genetic code as the adult sheep. The new cell began to divide and ultimately developed into a mature sheep, identical to the donor sheep. Thus, Dolly was a clone, an exact genetic replica of the sheep from which the original cell was taken.

The public outcry against the cloning process generally relates to the fear of the procedure being applied to humans. If this were accomplished, the clone and the person from whom the clone originated, like identical twins, would have the same chromosome portrait but would be separated in age by many years. The potential for organ donation, replacement of individuals lost in death, and selection and creation of a "super race" of identical individuals become real possibilities. Governments now debate the ethics of cloning but do not want to stifle scientific research.

Religious authorities have tended to denounce the procedure, declaring that cloning violates God's domain and authority. God entrusted His creation into the hands of humanity. God made people in His image and did not entrust them with absolute authority over human life, only over plant and animal life. Thus, cloning sheep or plants falls within our authority, while cloning humans does not. Plants and animals can be used to achieve human purposes, but other people should not be used in this way. People have a dignity by virtue of their being created in God's image (Gen. 1:27; 9:6). Another theological question is: Would the human clone have a soul? There is little reason to think not, since identical twins do. Few suspect that identical twins or triplets must share a soul and are thereby diminished.

While cloning does not require tampering with the genetic material, its attraction is found in the ability to produce a person with a particular genetic code. It represents a first step in a much larger enterprise of genetic design that itself is morally dubious. It is one thing to intervene medically or otherwise to help people, it is quite another thing to alter them without their consent to benefit someone else (see previous question). Producing a clone of a child, either to replace a child who has died or to donate bodily materials to help an ailing child, may seem noble at first glance. However, either action opens the door to a way of viewing and treating people (i.e., using them) as instruments rather than as unique individuals.

If we are going to justify cloning on the basis of how the clones produced can benefit other people—

i.e., on the basis of its consequences—then a broad range of consequences must be taken into account. Might not current research that has made it possible to produce headless mice make it tempting to produce headless human clones as a source of organs for transplantation? If human cloning could create a generation of individuals with desirable traits, might not others who are less desirable eventually be prevented—or at least hindered—from reproducing? Wouldn't we be inclined to change the world gene pool to suit our tastes and preferences? Why wouldn't the world powers be justified in repopulating the world with the race and traits they deem superior, dooming others to extinction? If attractive results justify using people, then there is no end to the possibilities.

Beyond all this, however, is the issue of developing the capability to clone humans safely. To produce the sheep clone, Dolly, there were 276 failed attempts, including the death of several defective clones. No one should subject a child to almost certain death through such experimentation no matter how much they want a child via cloning or otherwise.

22. Should I consider adoption instead?

Most couples do well to resolve their desire for biological offspring before attempting to adopt children. Pursuing adoption and assisted reproduction simultaneously proves to be very stressful emotionally and very draining financially.[6] Adoption, while legal, is by no means easy or predictable, and its cost may exceed $20,000. There are no guarantees. Though most adoptions do result in the gift of a child, there are too many cases where a biological mother changes her mind at or soon after the birth of the child. In light of the risks, adopting parents should pursue adoption cautiously while staying well informed as the process progresses. The loss of an adopted child—even one just recently adopted—can be as traumatic as the loss of one's biological child.

Adoption grafts a totally separate genetic line into a family. Adopting couples endure certain losses in the process. According to author Pat Johnston in *Adopting After Infertility*, infertile couples experience the loss of control, the loss of individual genetic continuity, the loss of a jointly conceived child, the loss of the pregnancy and birth experience, the loss of emotional experiences surrounding pregnancy and childbirth, and the loss of an opportunity to nurture and parent a new generation. Adoption resolves this last loss, but not the first five. Those considering adoption should remember that adoption may not meet all their needs or undo all their losses.[7]

Theologians considering the issue of adoption are generally supportive. They base their support on the biblical examples of Moses, Esther, and the adoptive process outlined in the New Testament by which believers become part of the family of God (Rom. 8:23). The decision to keep or place a child for adoption should be the sole responsibility of those who must provide for the child's care. Love for children includes concrete provision as well as emotional attachment. If the mother, father, or parents are unable to care for the child effectively, placing the child for adoption may be neither shameful nor immoral. Giving the child to parents who can meet the child's material and emotional needs can be a responsible act of love.

Nevertheless, adoption does separate the genetic

and rearing aspects of parenthood that are normally joined. The adoptive parents were not responsible for bringing the child into the world and, therefore, a weakened sense of responsibility of parents to child and child to parents could possibly result. As with other avenues of reproduction already discussed, children should not be intentionally conceived under circumstances in which the genetic parents will not be the rearing parents (see question 13). Nevertheless, once children have been conceived under circumstances that make it seemingly impossible for the genetic parents to rear them, two caring responses from other individuals or groups (e.g., church congregations) are appropriate. First, they can provide the encouragement and resources that despairing parents need to keep the children they have conceived. Second, when parents cannot or will not keep their children, others can adopt these children or help support people who are willing to do so. Adoption is a noble option under such circumstances.

An infant requires and deserves the best environment that can be provided. This applies equally regardless of race, genetic or physical deformity, or age. That every child should have a good home does not mean that any individual home can accommodate any particular child. When considering adoption, a couple should examine their beliefs, strengths, resources, and desires. Not every adoption situation fits every family situation. Some special-needs children, or children of particular backgrounds, may thrive only in homes with parents of special ability. Open adoption (not to be confused with shared parenting), where the birth parent knows and selects the adoptive situation, is generally considered to be the preferable arrangement by adoption agencies and social workers. However, closed adoptions, where the birth parent does not know the adopting parents, are also available.

Adoption offers a wonderful opportunity to parent a child(ren) in need of unconditional love and direction. Remember that a healthy family is the product of mutual love and commitment, whether or not a genetic link between parents and child exists.

Note, however, that an infertile couple's decision to adopt will not usually cause them to quickly conceive naturally. This common myth is debunked by the fact that only 5 percent of couples who adopt conceive naturally thereafter—the same percentage who conceive by simply dropping out of infertility treatment without adopting. Thus, the decision to adopt must be founded on a careful understanding of the process and the potential problems.

23. What are my legal concerns if I choose to adopt?

Laws regarding adoption vary greatly from state to state. A proposed Uniform Adoption Act, which would standardize state adoption laws, remains highly controversial. So for now, each state's specific requirements must be met for adoption within that state. If even a minor technicality is violated, the adoption may be revoked. These are general guidelines for a *nonrelated* (the adoptee is not biologically related to either adoptive parent) *domestic* (the child is born in the United States) adoption. *International* adoptions raise additional legal issues, such as emigration from the child's country of birth and immigration to the United States, but this book does not address the legal issues of international adoption. Adoptions can be handled either privately (by attorneys and the attending physician) or by an agency (government or private). However, some states prohibit private adoptions.

There are two discrete steps in any adoption. The first step is termination of the rights of the natural or presumed parents. This is where "due process concerns" (following constitutionally required procedures) are paramount. The termination of parental rights cannot be treated lightly. The birth mother must give her knowing, uncoerced consent. Consent of the biological father must be obtained, or adequate legal notice must be given.

The second step is the creation of a new parent-child relationship. Here, serious issues can develop when adopting parents try to undo this legally created relationship. For example, adoptive parents have sought to "return" a child who was diagnosed with Down's Syndrome, or ADHD (attention deficit hyperactive disorder), claiming they were not adequately informed of the child's medical history or risks.

Nonetheless, for a couple preparing to adopt, the procedures required by your state are spelled out clearly. You may be liable for your lawyer's fees and might not be able to recover payment for medical expenses if the adoption falls through. You must be approved as adoptive parents, and all states require that the adopter be an adult or at least a specific age of twenty-one or even older.

To finalize an adoption, parental rights (of the birth parents) must be terminated. Usually, this is based on their consent. The birth parents must sign a valid, "voluntary consent for adoption" form, no sooner than three to four days after birth (specified by state law). Some states permit parents to change their minds; others do not. The consent form allows the baby to be placed with the adoptive parents until the adoption is final.

If one of the birth parents did not sign a consent form, then his or her (usually the birth father's) parental rights must be terminated by court order for the adoption to proceed. This can be either voluntary or involuntary and in person or by legal document (the relinquishing parent does not have to appear in court). Standards for involuntary termination of parental rights vary from state to state.

The adoptive parents will file a petition for adoption; again, the waiting period varies from state to state. An in-home evaluation is conducted during this waiting period. If all the paperwork is complete and there are no objections (such as a birth father's claiming he was never notified), a final, irrevocable adoption order will be given by the court.

However, even a final adoption order can be reversed if the due-process rights of either birth parent were violated. In much publicized cases, such as the Baby Jessica and Baby Richard cases, custody of the child has been returned to the birth parents based on failure to comply with all aspects of applicable law, rather than on the "best interests of the child" standard. There is no agreement in the adoption or legal communities on defining the "best interests" of the child.

If the parents giving up or receiving the child are from different states, the requirements of the Interstate Compact should be consulted. It may be more complicated and expensive to do this through a private attorney rather than through an agency.

After an adoption is final, questions may arise regarding *inheritance* and *confidentiality of birth records*. Generally, a child may inherit from the adopting parents. Some states do not permit the child to inherit property limited to "heirs of one's body." Not all states permit the adopting parents to inherit from the child. Additional unresolved questions are whether the child may inherit from biological parents and whether the child and adoptive relatives other than adoptive parents may inherit from one another.

There is a heated debate within the adoption community about open records. Search organizations want access not only to medical information but also to information about birth parents. Adoption agencies argue that the threat of invasion of privacy by an adult biological child will deter adoption and encourage abortion.

Nonetheless, confidentiality of birth records is protected in nearly every state. Adoption records are sealed upon adoption and are available to the adult adoptee only by court order. Some states include provisions allowing birth parents absolute veto power over contacts requested by adoptees; others do not. Alaska, Hawaii, Kansas, and Tennessee have open adoption records; an adult adoptee can obtain the original, unamended birth certificate. Some states have active or passive reunion registries, which can facilitate contact if there is mutual interest between adoptee and birth parent.

24. How many children should we have?

There is no correct number of children that any particular couple should have. The mere fact that 15 percent of couples are infertile and so cannot have children apart from medical intervention renders any required number unachievable for many. The inherent failure rate in each of the contraceptive methods and the burgeoning unwanted-pregnancy rate in this country underscore the difficulty of controlling childbearing precisely. Besides, some people are well suited to the responsibilities of large families while others are not.

Societal pressures, financial circumstances, and personal preferences all influence people's decisions regarding childbearing and family size. Christians will often look to the Bible for guidance. Psalm 127:3 states: "Children are a gift of the LORD, the fruit of the womb is a reward." Some interpret this passage as a rejection of family planning, permanent sterilization, or other methods of limiting the evidence of God's blessing through childbearing. The biblical record does indeed support the idea that children often, though not always, are an evidence of God's pleasure. Thus, couples with this understanding, faced with infertility, will typically be open to considering whatever assisted techniques fit their belief systems (see question 9) and financial situations.

Others would argue, also from a Christian perspective, that children are *a* gift or heritage from the Lord, but *the* gift is Jesus Christ (John 3:16, Rom. 6:23). Thus, obedient service for them takes priority over biological reproduction. Following the commission (Matt. 28:19–20) to "make disciples," they desire to produce "spiritual offspring" by sharing the good news that people can be born again to a new life by committing themselves to Christ. Such persons may allow for divine direction in their lives regarding family size. Typically, they will pursue an approach to childbearing that consistently affirms rather than jeopardizes human life. They may note that just as God directs some to marry and some not to marry (in line with their different ministry responsibilities; 1 Cor. 7), so God directs people differently regarding childbearing.

Many take additional considerations into account, such as their responsibility to provide for the material and emotional needs of their children. Some even calculate the approximate cost of raising a child from infancy through the education process and make decisions based on income and expense. Others argue from the standpoint of world resources and maintain that concerned, educated couples will limit family size in order to limit the world's population growth. Adherents of this view see overpopulation as the reason why large portions of the earth's population are unable to obtain vital resources such as food, clean water, and medical care. Some countries have mandated maximum family size and require abortive procedures for pregnant women who have reached that limit. Because of these rigid restrictions, some couples have even decided to terminate pregnancies when the gender of the fetus is undesirable. Such developments illustrate the problems that arise when family size is limited by law, rather than left to the responsible judgment of each couple.

25. *What forms of contraception are effective in preventing pregnancy?*

Many contraceptive methods are currently available. They vary in effectiveness and in the way they work. For those who believe that any interference with the blessing of conception violates God's will, no methods of contraception (even a rhythm method) may be employed. Many Christian couples, however, plausibly maintain that God can and will guide them in the proper exercise and timing of childbearing (see previous question).

Rhythm methods. Some couples consider the use of any chemical or technological form of contraception to be unnatural and, therefore, ungodly. The only acceptable way for them to avoid pregnancy is the rhythm method, which involves abstaining from sexual intercourse during the period each month when the wife is most likely to get pregnant. They identify this period by measuring fluctuations in the wife's body temperature and/or cervical mucus.

How effective is the rhythm method? The effectiveness of contraceptive methods is determined by "hundred women years' use." That is, if one hundred women used a particular technique for one year, how many would get pregnant? For comparison, roughly 80 percent of couples using no means of contraception will conceive within the year. By using the rhythm method of periodic abstinence structured by the temperature and cervical mucus changes, 10 percent to 15 percent will conceive in one year's time.

Barrier methods. A second approach to preventing pregnancy involves techniques that strive to prevent sperm from reaching the egg by mechanical and/or chemical means. These techniques include condoms, diaphragms with spermicidal agents, cervical caps, and the female condom. They are approximately as effective in preventing pregnancy as the rhythm method.

The pill. For a more effective approach to contraception, some couples turn to birth control pills. Oral contraceptives are designed primarily to prevent ovulation or egg release. Most pills are combinations of an estrogen and a progesterone derivative that regulate a woman's menstrual cycle artificially—generally without allowing egg maturation and release. The pill is quite effective at preventing pregnancy, with approximately one pregnancy per "hundred women years' use." Correct pill usage (daily, at approximately the same time each day) is necessary for the pill to be this effective in preventing ovulation.

The pill's reliability is also affected by the altered absorption of the pill hormones that can occur when the woman becomes ill and/or takes medications. In addition to preventing ovulation, the pill thickens the cervical mucus, making sperm penetration more difficult. The pill also changes the motion of the cilia (tiny hairlike structures) within the fallopian tubes, altering egg transport. A final effect of the pill is that it thins the uterine lining, making the lining less favorable to implantation should fertilization occur, thereby causing the embryo to die. This effect is more frequent in pills that contain only progesterone rather than the progesterone/estrogen combination. Progesterone-only pills are more likely to allow ovulation, increasing the possibility that a fertilized egg will reach the uterus and try to implant there.

Norplant. Another contraception method using sustained-released low-dose progesterone is the Norplant system. Small, needle-shaped implants are placed just below the skin. These release prescribed amounts of progesterone to prevent ovulation. This technique is also very effective contraceptively, but side effects including unpredictable spotting can cause patient dissatisfaction.

Sterilization. Sterilization is a procedure that makes the body incapable of producing a child through sexual intercourse. Multiple procedures are currently available that can achieve this end. Some are reversible, others much less so; however, with the existence of so many forms of assisted reproductive technology today, a range of options for achieving pregnancy is always present.

In the female, tubal sterilization is the most common procedure. It involves tying, cauterizing, clipping, or using some other means of interrupting the fallopian tube to prevent the sperm from reaching the egg. Ovaries still produce hormones cyclically and eggs are released. They are simply not exposed to sperm except in rare instances of procedure failure. Additionally, removal of the ovaries (bilateral oophorectomy) or removal of the uterus (hysterectomy) will similarly make conception unlikely through normal means. However, expense and surgical risk generally make these less appropriate forms of sterilization.

In the male, sterilization generally involves interrupting the vas deferens, the tube that transports the sperm from the testicle to the storage area (the seminal vesicles, just below the prostate gland). Usually the surgeon will remove a small portion of the vas, tying off the remaining ends. This procedure is called vasectomy.

Sterilization procedures have some risk. Whereas local anesthesia is sufficient for a vasectomy, the other forms of sterilization require general anesthesia, which carries a larger though still small risk. Some women report cycle irregularity and heightened menstrual pain following tubal surgery. There may also be a link between vasectomy and some immunological problems. These possibilities should be investigated with the counsel of a qualified specialist.

26. Are there other forms of contraception?

In question 8, we discussed the embryo. There we noted the difference between fertilization (when the new person comes into being) and implantation (when the embryonic person attaches to the mother's uterus for support. We also noted that the word *conception* generally refers to the moment of fertilization. However, some people use the word *conception* differently to refer to the point when the embryo (the new life) is first physically attached to the mother, i.e., implantation. According to this different definition, anything that acts to block implantation (i.e., prevent the embryo from attaching to the uterus) would be a form of contraception.

We reject the use of the term in this way because it implies that human life does not begin until implantation. People who recognize that a new human being is present at fertilization will identify those contraceptives that prevent implantation to be a form of abortion rather than contraception. Such contraceptives prevent the embryonic person already conceived from implanting—resulting in the death of the embryo.

The IUD. Somewhat more effective than rhythm and barrier methods is the IUD, or intrauterine device. IUDs are pieces of plastic of assorted shapes that are inserted into the uterine cavity to remain over a period of time. Some contain the hormone (progesterone) while others contain copper, an element that statistically heightens the effectiveness.

Exactly how IUDs do work is currently hotly debated. Historically, people have believed that the IUD acts by allowing fertilization but preventing the embryo from implanting in the uterus. Thus, the theory has been that the IUD generates a uterine environment hostile to the approaching embryo. Recent and ongoing research raises the possibility that the IUD may also prevent fertilization by disrupting sperm function within the uterus.

This research is not yet convincing and requires further studies with larger trial groups. Small group laparoscopic studies have failed to detect viable sperm in the fallopian tubes of women with IUDs in place. This would suggest that an IUD directly affects sperm in addition to creating a hostile intrauterine environment. How often the IUD truly prevents conception and how often it aborts an embryo remains unclear. Some physicians do continue to place IUDs after intercourse as a morning-after approach to guard against pregnancy—reflecting their confidence in its abortifacient effect.

The IUD, however it works, is quite successful in preventing ongoing pregnancy with failure rates in the range of two to four per "hundred women years' use." A woman using an IUD must consider the slight risk of intrauterine infection leading to infertility, perforation of the uterus, or spontaneous passing of the device without her knowledge.

The morning-after pill. Once sexual intercourse has occurred, it is too late to prevent the sperm from reaching the egg. If fertilization occurs, the only way to keep a pregnancy from proceeding is to prevent implantation. To accomplish this, a woman can take pills containing high doses of a hormone within forty-eight hours following intercourse. The treatment disrupts the intrauterine environment such that if fertilization does occur, implantation is very unlikely. Blocking implantation provides a way to abort the embryo when adequate contraceptive measures were not in place, e.g., in situations of rape, incest, and casual sex.

RU-486 and similar drugs. Abortifacient drugs such as RU-486 and its derivatives are used by some as a form of birth control (as opposed to contraception). They provide ways to get rid of the embryo or fetus before birth but after conception and implantation. These medicines work by blocking the ovary's production of progesterone, the hormone crucial for intrauterine survival during the early weeks of pregnancy. If this hormone is blocked, the pregnancy will spontaneously abort. RU-486 and its derivatives can even terminate a pregnancy several months along. This option can be exercised at home without surgery. There is, however, a risk of failure or incomplete abortion. This approach is legal in Europe and as of this writing appears likely to become legal very soon in the United States as well. These drugs are hard to limit in any case because they typically have uses other than abortion.

27. Is it okay to use any form of birth control?

The first decisions to make are whether or not to have sexual intercourse (see question 7) and whether or not to exercise any influence on the timing and number of children that may result (see question 24). For those who consider it moral to be sexually active and to use some form of birth control, there are three types of intervention to consider. First are the true forms of contraception—those that actually prevent conception.

Methods that prevent conception include rhythm methods, barrier methods, the pill, Norplant, and sterilization. Apart from the exception noted below, they are respectful of life by acting before a new human being comes into existence at conception. Nevertheless, to determine if it is right for you to use any of them, you should consider issues of financial cost, comfort, effectiveness, and other pragmatic concerns such as those raised in question 25.

There are two additional issues concerning the rhythm method that must be addressed. First, is there a valid distinction between contraceptive practices, which some believe thwart God's reproductive purposes, and the rhythm method? Is not the use of the rhythm method also an attempt to alter the natural consequences of sexual intercourse in marriage? Second, rhythm methods require couples to abstain from sexual intercourse for more than a brief period of time. Couples may want to consider the admonition of 1 Corinthians 5:7 regarding the wisdom of such abstinence.

Barrier methods raise no additional concerns as long as people are under no illusions that they provide complete protection from either sexually transmitted diseases or pregnancy. However, use of the pill requires further comment. As explained in question 25, there is more than one kind of pill. Pills that contain only progesterone are more likely to allow ovulation to occur and then to abort the embryo by blocking implantation. Those who recognize abortion as morally unacceptable (see question 8) will avoid this type of pill. Whether the multiple-hormone pills pose a significant risk of causing abortion by blocking implantation is debatable; more research is needed to answer this vital question. However, it is better established that a woman can maximize the ability of such pills to block ovulation and conception by taking them at the same time each day and avoiding intercourse during illness, especially while on other medications. She can also resist the temptation to minimize the dosage of estrogen. Reducing estrogen may be attractive in order to reduce its unpleasant side effects; however, doing so increases the dangers described above in relation to the progesterone pill. Consult your physician.

The last truly contraceptive approach, sterilization, also raises special issues. Is it right to sacrifice the ability to reproduce and, if so, when and under what conditions? Some would argue that any intervention that obstructs evidence of divine favor (i.e., the provision of any further children) is immoral. They question why anyone would try to prevent the outpouring of love from God by disrupting the divine plan for "holy offspring."

Others would argue that the divine imperative to be fruitful and multiply, filling the earth (Gen. 2), has already been accomplished. In any case, they would add, this mandate does not delineate how many children a couple should have. They believe that God has endowed His creatures with insight and divine principles of guidance that permit individual assessment of needs, resources, and goals, thus opening the door to consider sterilization when the "right number" of children has been born. Those open to sterilization may also argue that God will hold men and women accountable not for their families' numerical size, but for how they care for their families.

In any case, two cautions are in order. First, sterilization is a personal matter. Under no circumstances should it be legally imposed against a person's wishes. In the case of mentally incompetent persons whose wishes are not known, anyone responsible for acting on their behalf must act in the best interest of those persons. Second, to the degree that it is irreversible —or might be—it is morally problematic in that it renders one unable to exercise the God-given ability to have children should circumstances change (e.g., the tragic death of one's children or spouse).

The other two types of birth control include those interventions that prevent implantation (e.g., the IUD and the morning-after pill) or birth (e.g., RU-486). Their greatest moral flaw is that they both entail abortion (though see also question 26 regarding the IUD). Whether or not we recognize the pre-implantation embryo or the more developed embryo or fetus as a human being to be protected depends on our view of the issues discussed in question 8. These are not merely theoretical or academic issues. Whether we want to face them or not, these issues ultimately cannot be avoided. They are inescapable matters of life and death.

Human reproductive technologies and approaches can be wonderful gifts—by overcoming infertility and helping to shape family planning—as long as they don't destroy life in the process.

Conclusion

Advances in reproductive technology generate new opportunities that generate new ethical concerns. Making correct choices demands a clear and precise understanding of each new medical procedure. Theological principles supply foundational support and direction to guide our thinking. Whether people choose to believe it or not, we *are* created in the image of God.

The manner in which we treat ourselves and the embryos we produce is important to our Creator and should reflect His concern and care for human life. He has gifted us with the curiosity and intellect to seek out technologies that improve human health and well-being, but we must be mindful to use them unselfishly within the boundaries of love. We must live with a genuine sense of responsibility to God, to ourselves, and to the children with whom we are blessed.

Recommended Reading

The Center for Bioethics and Human Dignity Resources:

Cameron, Nigel M. de S., ed. *Embryos and Ethics.* Edinburgh, Scotland: Rutherford House, 1987.

The Center for Bioethics and Human Dignity. *The Reproduction Revolution.* A series of audio tapes, videos, and a book. Forthcoming in early 1999.

Other Resources:

"Donum Vitae" [an exposition of the Roman Catholic position]. *Origins* 16, no. 40 (19 March 1987): 698–710.

Evans, Debra. *Without Moral Limits: Women, Reproduction and the New Medical Technology.* Westchester, Ill.: Crossway, 1989.

Feinberg, John S., and Paul D. Feinberg. *Ethics for a Brave New World.* Wheaton, Ill.: Crossway, 1993.

O'Donovan, Oliver. *Begotten or Made?* New York: Oxford University Press, 1984.

Rae, Scott B. *Brave New Families: Biblical Ethics and Reproductive Technologies.* Grand Rapids: Baker, 1996.

Endnotes

1. For the biblical accounts, see Genesis 16, 17, and 21 for Sarah; Judges 13 for Samson's mother; 1 Samuel 1 and 2 for Hannah; and Luke 1 for Elizabeth.
2. For more information on the role of sexuality and marriage, see *Sexual Intimacy in Marriage* by William Cutrer and Sandra Glahn (Grand Rapids: Kregel Publications, 1998).
3. See Deuteronomy 25:5–10 for provisions under the Mosaic Law regarding levirate marriage. Perhaps the most well-known levirate marriage in the Bible is that of Ruth and Boaz who appear in the family line of Jesus in Matthew 1.
4. See *Chicago Tribune,* 11 September 1997; 20 November 1997 and Joan Beck, "Careless Intentions: Have We Fully Thought Out All of the Consequences of Reproductive Medicine?", February 1998, Commentary section.
5. See Robert Jay Litfin, *The Nazi Doctors: Medical Killing and the Psychology of Genocide* (New York: Basic Books, 1986).
6. For more information on the issues facing couples in regard to infertility, see *When Empty Arms Become a Heavy Burden* by Sandra Glahn and William Cutrer (Nashville: Broadman and Holman, 1997).
7. Pat Johnson, *Adopting After Infertility* (Indianapolis: Perspectives Press, 1992).